Smart Boundaries

How To Set Personal and Emotional Boundaries for Mental Health Development

Usama Cheema

no scenarios in which the publisher or the original author of this work can be in any fashion deemed liable for any hardship or damages that may befall them after undertaking information described herein.

Additionally, the information in the following pages is intended only for informational purposes and should thus be thought of as universal. As befitting its nature, it is presented without assurance regarding its prolonged validity or interim quality. Trademarks that are mentioned are done without written consent and can in no way be considered an endorsement from the trademark holder.

CONTENTS

BORDERS FOR A BOUNTIFUL LIFE

Although imperceptible with the naked eye, our vibrant boundaries mean the difference between experiencing joyful, prosperous and loving lives, or experiencing sadness, finite and unhappy pain. They separate what we need from what we don't need, and selectively put into our lives only those energies, people, guidance, thoughts, situations, opportunities, and treatments that bring our spiritual essence into real life. . They also go further, purposefully seeking and absorbing everything needed to realize our hopes and dreams.

Our vibrant borders border our spiritual selves and promote our nature, which is one of the reasons I often call them "spiritual borders." We are eager to express this inner identity, and establishing the right energy boundary will help us do this. If created and managed correctly, they will ensure that our true selves (and not our thoughts, thoughts and beliefs) are in charge of our lives. They share information with the world, tell everyone who we are, what we want and how they treat us.

Maybe you don't even know that you need to make invisible parameters to protect your safety and integrity. As you read this book, you will find that not only do you have to have these boundaries, but having them will greatly improve your life. You will rely on the new "force field" so that you will not leave your home or go home unless you open it.

Those of us who lack borders or whose borders are damaged are often preyed by predators: those who use us intentionally or unintentionally; situations that cause us to fall over and over again; depressing behavior patterns that make us feel happier than we should be, love , Support, satisfaction, respect and provide less. It's very simple. There are no boundaries. We cannot share our identity with the world. We will not get the bounty provided by the world. The symptoms of energetic boundary problems range from irritating to traumatic. They can include:

- Feeling overwhelmed by other people's feelings, emotions, needs, problems, negative emotions and even illness

- Habitual people usually harm their own interests and suddenly cause negative effects

- Carrying and caring about other people and feeling tired, angry and frustrated, but getting nothing

- Recurring money, relationships and work dilemmas

- Weight loss and physical illness are the result of absorbing external energy

- Fear and distraction caused by intrusive psychological or supernatural events or energies

- Generalized Anxiety Disorder, which is the product of invisible dangers that always require attention

- Constant coercion is often a symptom of the energy and needs of others, rather than our own

- The embarrassment of your behavior does not reflect your true self and makes you tolerate the absurdity of others

- Except you, everyone feels naive to the universe or the existence of God

In my intuitive consulting practice, at least two-thirds of people I have met lack energetic boundaries or impaired boundaries.

However, by erecting and/or repairing these boundaries, they have developed into a leapfrog development.

A woman who had been unemployed for two years got three jobs in one month. A good-looking young man who had not been in contact for five years met a woman within a week. Six months later, he wrote to me and told me that they are now living happily together. (Yes, happiness!)

A young mother with three autism or Attention Deficit Disorder (ADD) – Spectrum Kids reported that she was able to stay calm, and all three children she had helped set the boundaries of energetic are now in "normal school".

A child who cannot sleep can suddenly sleep all night. Her teddy bear and "the terrible thing under the bed" stopped talking to her. An old man with amyotrophic lateral sclerosis (ALS) changed his condition and began to live asymptomatically.

Everyone has a greater ability to make more satisfying decisions. Avoid or change bad energy conditions; establish and maintain healthy relationships; create more wealth and abundance; eliminate or reduce addiction, depression or anxiety tendencies;

identify and follow their intuition; and enjoy the best life. I know that whenever an appropriate energy boundary is generated, not only will I feel better, but my life will also be improved. People treat me better. I was shocked by the bright insight before me. The words I need flow through me. My parents' upbringing has improved. I will attract money or opportunities that are struggling with happiness in struggle. My health has improved, or at least for health reasons, I have found a solution. I can even make more effective stock and investment decisions because I can reconcile the negative emotions of others and stick to my inner wisdom.

Setting healthy, energetic boundaries for yourself will take some work, but the effort is worth it. Each stage of work increases your exposure to light and joy, and reduces your exposure to sources of negativity and exhaustion. The ultimate goal is to align your spiritual boundaries and make them more elegantly reflect your true spiritual nature. This consistency ensures that every level and level of your life can absorb supporting energy and avoid negative energy.

Before the specific introduction, we will briefly discuss the purpose, formation and function of the energy boundary. We will also investigate 7 boundary syndromes, which are common conditions caused by missing or damaged energy boundaries. I will help you identify the syndromes that may inhibit you. This discussion will help you identify the cause of boundary problems, so that you know how to better change the boundary. Throughout the process, exercises will help you establish healthy mental boundaries. After reading this book, you will be able to safely build and create a full and rich life.

Finally, to establish our energetic boundaries is to take the life we have always known to have, the life we are ready to share with our loved ones, and the stable life in the divine grace. This is the life we dream of; this is the way we guarantee our lives through healthy, vibrant boundaries.

OUR FOUR ENERGETIC BOUNDARIES

> *"No" is a complete sentence.*
>
> ANNE LAMOTT

Think of our vibrant borders as border patrols. These guards are our internal procedures and they have three basic functions:

- **Providing protection.** They exclude energy that cannot support our spiritual essence.

- **Filtering.** They emit energy that strengthens our spiritual essence, retain the energy we need, and emit energy or information that maintains our world.

- **Magnetizing.** They have absorbed what we need, including treatment, information, guidance, people, events, work, money, healthy relationships, life lessons, etc.

As mentioned in Chapter 1, there are many types of energy boundaries around our bodies, but the main one is the golden light field. As we grow, our spirit activates age-appropriate golden layers or vibrant boundaries, and inspires it with spiritual truths or procedures that clearly and gracefully suit our unique selves. Unfortunately, our spirit is not the only influence on these boundaries. Our parents, relatives, ancestors, schools, religious institutions, friends, enemies, colleagues, bosses, news sources and the entire culture also have their own say, for better or worse. Life events ranging from long-term negative effects to one-time trauma can also prevent our boundaries from developing or maintaining harmony with our true spiritual essence.

When our borders are violated, there are three basic positive effects:

- **Our boundaries become rigid or immobilized.** Think about the cold wall. Being close to it makes us and others feel cold and shut down. The rigid energy boundary has the same effect. People are far away, feeling that we are unavailable or not interested in them. Fixed boundaries also exclude potentially positive events or opportunities: investments, promotions or new jobs, healing energy, referrals to the right healthcare professionals, friendships that may make us heartwarming, children's love and trust. When these positive people and experiences are constantly being abandoned, we will eventually feel lonely and alienated.

- **Our boundaries become permeable.** The permeation boundary is loose and fragile. Imagine fighting with a soft cloth instead of a sword. You will last what? About ten seconds on the battlefield. People with permeable boundaries are push-ups. They are easily thrown away, ignored, used, exploited or not rewarded.

- **Our boundaries are sliced, diced, and cut full of holes.** The gap of our energy boundary leaves a gap in our lives, at the door, anyone and anyone can pass through it. We can easily absorb the energy of others, from disease to poverty, and lose our own life force. The more troubled the problems in our lives, the more likely we are to have loopholes in the energy field. Any of these conditions will cause any of the seven energy syndromes that we will discuss in the next chapter.

Each of our twelve auroral layers has a different function and is essential to our health and well-being. For example, the innermost layer closest to our skin can regulate our relationship with gender, money, professional achievement, and your basic safety needs. The green band corresponding to the field and center of our relationship is connected with love, change and inner attention. The outer layer, which I think is gold, extends to heaven, bringing spiritual magic into our daily lives.

According to my study, professional practice and personal life, I divide the twelve layers or boundaries into four types according to work or function, and associate each type with a specific color:

- Physical (red) boundaries

- Emotional(orange) boundaries

- Relational (green) boundaries

- Spiritual (white) boundaries

Within each of these boundaries are subsets of other colors. For example, gold and silver are members of the white family, while yellow belongs to the emotional family. I will discuss the specific layers and their functions in Chapter 4. Now, let us take the rainbow road and find out what happens in each energy boundary category, if each one is healthy, how our life will look, and how to compromise.

Your Physical Energy Boundaries: Red at the Crossings

What do you think when you focus on red? Life, love, excitement, lover, blood, fire, racing, wounds. Red is associated with the body, it is related to the richness of being a physical existence and the ups and downs associated with it.

The job of the red boundary is to ensure our personal safety and to inspire us to move towards physical success. This is to screen out situations that may jeopardize our safety and potential victory, and enhance or attract our positive situation. Our red border enhances our physical health by enhancing all our basic needs (including health conditions). They ensure that we have a safe and warm living place; clothing that suits our lifestyle and goals; as well as fresh air, clean water and healthy food. They assured us of partnership, which can include romance, maintenance, sexual satisfaction and sweet spousal relationships.

Our red border ensures that we have money and financial stability. However, true financial security is not only about having enough money to pay the bills, it also requires investing some extra money. This involves knowing that our money is the tail of the kite for career or work. We are here to contribute to this world. We have contributed to this world. Financial compensation is only part of the formula. We should make a difference through our efforts and be recognized for this.

If we are physically insecure, we will not be able to enjoy relationships, money, career or sex, or even food and dream house. As a means of personal safety, we and our loved ones are protected from serious diseases, abuse, addiction or threats to our material and physical health, and as far as possible from their harm. Personal safety is one of the most important blessings of our red border, because without it, we will not be able to enjoy other blessings.

But even if we have strong physical boundaries, life will have its dangers and problems. We always have to learn lessons. For example, safety is essentially an inner achievement, not an outer achievement. However, to have good energetic boundaries, please make sure that when life is in the ups and downs, we are not always at the shaky end.

What Compromises Our Physical Energy Boundaries?

Unfortunately, many situations and conditions impose on our physical energy boundaries. Everyone has their own energetic list of problems that can cause any of the seven syndromes described in the next chapter. Some of the injuries that cause rigid, permeable or open boundaries and physical energy issues are. At the top of the list are physical violations, such as involvement in an accident or injury.

The blow to the body immediately takes effect on our vibrant borders. These border injuries can be cured, but not always. Although we may suffer long-term physical injuries due to injuries (car accidents can cause us to lose limbs, sports injuries can cause us to lose the life of a leg), if the following happens, we will not incur other consequences, such as other injuries or Our energetic borders can completely repair themselves. But if our energetic borders still break, we will experience any of the seven syndromes.

For example, one of my clients had a serious car accident when she was 16 years old. When their mother and sister were blinded by a drunk driver, she was driving with her mother and sister as passengers. My client's mother was killed immediately, and her sister was paralyzed from the waist. My client escaped the accident with only a slight twist, and it didn't even show up on the X-ray film. She called me when she was thirty-six. She was desperate. She had consulted doctors and received medical treatment. Whenever she wanted to do something beneficial to her, such as asking for a raise or taking a vacation, her neck would cramp so terribly that she had to cancel the plan. Not only that, but every time someone asks her for help, unless she is unwilling to perform the task, she will feel the same pain, even if she doesn't want to. From cleaning the house to making dinner for him and his new wife, his father was particularly good at getting her to obey orders.

My client felt guilty about the car accident, which made her feel that she not only had to constantly atone for her sins but also denied her grace and kindness. The feeling of lack of self-forgiveness is like a wedge that keeps the vibrant boundaries of her body unable to close. Unfortunately, others, especially her father, learned how to slip out of this hole and asked her to meet their needs at the expense of her own interests. When my client learned how to close the hole and open up her heart to herself, the vibrant border filled her neck pain and stopped completely. She also learned that responsibility begins with taking care of herself.

Being sexually, physically, emotionally, and/or mentally abused makes us struggle for pain, and pain only intensifies as we change in physical strength. I have worked with about 20,000 clients who were treated horribly as children, raped or abused as adults, or helplessly witnessed the same treatment of others.

Any abuse (whether it happens to us once or multiple times, whether it happens to us or we see it happen to others), will create loopholes in the physical field, which may lead to any or all of the discussions in the next chapter Syndrome. It will also affect the other three boundaries, making them rigid, permeable or full of pores. Chapters 5 to 8 discuss solutions to energetic problems caused by abuse.

People usually think that as long as they witnessed the abuse, they were not really injured. Since they have not been abused themselves, how can they encounter the same problems as the abuse? The reason is largely dynamic. Children usually cannot be distinguished from others. They cannot tell where their own boundaries begin, and where the boundaries of others end. Therefore, they can personalize what others are going through. For example, if children see someone being beaten, they will vigorously absorb the strength of the blow. If it happens only once, the physical boundaries of their injuries may be restored. However, repeated occurrences will permanently destroy the physical boundaries of children. As a result, they will later attract partners who want to get rid of energy by hitting others, or the children themselves will grow up to get rid of negative energy by hitting others.

Children are particularly vulnerable to mothers. One of the reasons is that they have kept in touch with their mothers at least through their three-year-old umbilical cord energy line. The mother's experience was passed on to her children almost directly through the rope. Any problems that the mother is unwilling or unable to solve, such as abuse, illness and addiction, are also full of vitality. This energy may also include problematic emotions, thoughts, and spiritual beliefs, which may damage the child's other three boundaries.

One of the reasons why children's energetic boundaries absorb the energy of others is that children are innocent. They love. They have not given up on their inner heart, which is the part of our body that produces the most energy. Children will not absorb the negative and hurt themselves from others. They do this because they love and want to help their loved ones.

In the final analysis, harmful forces are actual energy that can produce physical effects. They can stay in our energy boundaries forever, or at least stay in our energy boundaries until they are gently eliminated through healing and energetic methods. The gulf they create on the boundaries of energetic bodies can't help but cause the same treatment we experienced when we first abused it.

Do you think you cannot actively contract the disease? Think again. Experiencing long-term illnesses of ourselves or others may make us vulnerable to illnesses and plights of others, that is, until we close the vulnerability gap in the energy boundaries of the body. A client of mine was diagnosed with thirty diseases in his lifetime, from leukemia to shingles. guess what? Her mother has been sick throughout her growing up. My client's condition improved after closing the physically active border.

Any traumatic physical, emotional or relationship violations, such as being abandoned, unnecessary, neglected, overworked, or chronically impoverished, can damage our physical boundaries. For example, one of my clients lost his mother in his early years. My client became a shopaholic, but interestingly, she only bought red clothes. It turns out that her mother loves red and always wore a red dress when she was killed in a car accident. After my client dealt with the abandonment issue, her consumer frenzy ended.

I also worked with a 15-year-old girl whose mother tried to abort her seven times. The energy boundary of the girl's body was pierced so many times by the attempted miscarriage that she has no physical energy boundary of any kind. This girl absolutely did everything anyone asked her. If her friends tried cocaine, she would do it. If others drop classes, she will. If someone wants her to do homework, then do it. By the age of 15, she had been wandering around, making love to make money, and buying drugs for her friends.

She has been working with the therapist, but nothing has changed until I carried a doll with me for a week. Her job is to dress the doll in red and take care of it. After playing with the doll for a week, my client refused to have sex with her newest boyfriend. She moved to her aunt's house, transferred to another school, and started to work hard to get A's direct department.

Even mental violations can destroy our physical limits. For example, I once worked with a client who was tortured by the spirit of ancestors. This ancestor was addicted to gin when he was alive, and now his spirit is transmitted to my client as a voice, forcing him to drink against his will every night, so that he can get drunk through my client's drinking. This spirit takes advantage of my client's upbringing and original trauma, including being beaten by my own drunk father, and entering the realm of my client's physical energy. We took the spirit away and blocked the hole. And, don't force it anymore!

An emerging field called epigenetics reveals another way of looking at our physical energetics. Epigenetics is the study of the chemical "soup" surrounding our genes. This soup contains memories and imprints of our ancestors. If our great-grandfather lost the family farm and determined that he failed, then we can inherit his failure syndrome. From poverty to mental illness, what a generation can experience can continue and determine which genes are switched or turned off or turned on. From our DNA and cells. This means that through the areas of our various units, our ancestors may tell people how to react to us.

Another important area of research, called microchimerism, has proven that our mother's cells live in our body for a long time after we escape from the placenta. In fact, many people still live their lives. If these cells get along well with our cells, they can strengthen our immune system, leaving us with nowhere to escape from diabetes to cancer. If these cells are not suitable for us, our body will attack them and cause us to suffer from many diseases. I believe that, like all cells, mother cells emit their own energy fields, and these energy fields produce physical reactions in our bodies.

In short, all types of physical invasion can cause problems by inducing or exacerbating damage to ourselves and destroying our physical field. Any or all of the seven syndromes can evolve from the cracks we leave in the energetic areas of the body.

Your Emotional Energy Boundaries: Orange You Glad You're Happy?

Orange is the color of our emotional boundaries. It leads us to happy opportunities and to get rid of misfortune. They enable us to transform so-called negative emotions (such as fear, sadness, disgust, and anger) into joy. They motivate us to adopt attitudes and actions that will mature us through all our life experiences (for good or for bad).

Emotion is a combination of belief and emotion. The reason they are described as orange is because in the energy system, red represents deep feelings or sensations, and yellow represents our thoughts. Put these two together and you will get orange, which is a combination of two interdependent ways of knowledge and experience.

Belief is the perception of reality. Feeling is information from our body. Beliefs tell us what we should feel, and our feelings tell us how to deal with our beliefs. When we are in reaction mode, it is difficult to figure out what started this process, but if we have a fully functional, healthy emotional energy boundary, then life will become easier. At least, they provide us with the time we need to experience our feelings, recognize the important information provided by our feelings, and think through our reactions. This emotional buffer ensures that our response to life stimuli enhances our lives and does not harm ourselves or others.

For example, suppose your mother tells you that you cannot bring other important people to a festive meal. You will feel angry and disrespectful. Because you have strong emotional energy boundaries, you know that your anger is not your mother's; it is your own. You know her actions are more than you said. You can respect angry messages instead of overreacting, that is, telling you that you need protective boundaries or space to make decisions based on your own value system (rather than mother's problems). Anger will also alert you to your own values and tell you that you should be respected. In response, maybe you tell your mother that you want to come to eat, as long as your partner can do too. Or maybe you suggest that your mother come to your home, where you, her and your important partner can celebrate together.

Rigid, permeable or huge emotional boundaries will mess up your feelings and thinking. You may not make yourself angry with your mother's ban, but you will probably freeze one of three fear-based reactions because of the border damage: freeze, fight, or run away.

Maybe you told yourself that you have no right to be angry with anyone, especially your mother, so you freeze and tell yourself that for the sake of your mother's peace, you will agree to your mother's request. You can justify your policeman by thinking that other people who are important shouldn't put your place on her holiday table, because being one more person will be tiring, or the vacation is just a family member and no outsider time, or It's just "um", mother always knows best. "Maybe you will be vague for other important people and pretend to be sick during the holidays so that you can sneak up to your mother. Your own guilt will then cause you to get angry with your partner at some point. From the energy point of view In other words, this explosion will pour the anger you should have directed against your mother on your loved one.

On the other hand, maybe you will fight and tell your mother that you will never talk to her again. This knee-jerk reaction is an unhealthy substitute and cannot replace feelings and explain your own feelings and needs. Another typical reaction is to run away. It's time to book that ticket to Cancun, leave your important relatives and mother behind, right? wrong. Responding to fear, rather than feeling and then making a decision, will only increase our agitation and renew the damage of our vibrant borders. These reactions will not benefit anyone, including you.

WHAT COMPROMISES OUR EMOTIONAL ENERGETIC BOUNDARIES?

What broke our emotional boundaries? The main reasons are our low mood, absorbing the emotions of others and holding immature beliefs. These situations can cause us to fall into a rigid emotional energy state, which makes us feel lonely in the world and lose contact with ourselves. Permeable boundaries make us crazy and unstable emotions; and well-defined boundaries, which may make us emotionally overwhelmed and exhausted.

"Feeling at a discount" refers to when others or we should not feel or not feel our feelings. This kind of experience, especially the long-term experience, makes us feel that we are not counted and seem to be worthless. In most cases, we can exempt someone from disregarding our feelings without permanently damaging our inner or emotional energy boundaries. If the bank teller doesn't smile at us, we can assume that she has a bad or impolite life. Everything with a smile on her face has nothing to do with us. However, some negligence can cause the wound to be deeper and last longer. If others, especially those we love, do not, it is difficult for us to cherish our or our own feelings.

Consistent cruelty, ridicule, humiliation, accusations, "internal gui" or negligence also force us to respond to our vibrant boundaries. They may become thick walls to protect us, or they may become permeable membranes to hide our hurt feelings. Otherwise, they may not be able to keep up with the problem of fixing the huge gap caused by the incoming negative factors, simply because such negative effects will never destroy them.

If we spend too much time on people who are unwilling and unable to deal with their feelings, our emotional vitality boundary will be destroyed. Sometimes other people deny their feelings and let us feel these emotions, so they don't have to. To make matters worse, some people squeeze their emotions into our bodies, penetrate our energetic boundaries, and leave us at a loss and confusion.

I often see physical damage to emotional energy between men and women in major relationships. Most commonly, this man has never been confirmed or counted when he grows up. As a result, he feels sad or sad. However, showing that being hurt or sad is not considered a masculine thing; he is easy to get angry and more acceptable. The anger gradually accumulates and it feels bad. The energy needs to go somewhere, and eventually it breaks through the man's own emotional energy boundary, creating a huge hole or escaping through an existing exit. Usually, the external result is a series of hurtful speech, even physical violence, although sometimes men will defuse anger and turn it into passive aggressive behavior.

For example, they may agree to help their spouse with a project, but forget the due date, or promise to pick up the child from the daycare, and then "be very busy." In both cases, their other important party is forced to deal with the crisis. The farther he gets from real feelings such as sadness, injury, or disappointment, the harder it is for him to listen to his true feelings and react to the situation honestly rather than passively. Short- and long-term consequences include illness and stress (caused by accumulated emotions), poor decision-making, and injury or relationship breakdown.

Men's female partners often absorb anger into their emotional energy boundaries. Women usually grow up to take care of the needs of others. Other people's emotions penetrate into their own shields when they are young, forming holes or permeable membranes. Unknowingly, their energetic boundaries declared: "Here, here! I can take care of your anger." Therefore, a woman will experience pain or injury to vent her anger and release her love energy.

In the body, spiritual or subtle energy can be transformed into physical energy through chakras, which can transform physical energy into spiritual energy and vice versa. From psychotoxins to physical toxins, it can cause or intensify inflammation. Inflammation is the cause of dozens of diseases, including chronic fatigue syndrome, arthritis, heart disease, and even cancer. Ignoring one's own feelings and embracing the shame of others' feelings may also increase a woman's existing feelings of self-disgust or low self-worth. Poor self-image can lead to other problems, including anorexia, overeating, addictive or compulsive behaviors, such as excessive drinking or shopping.

These problems may also include many less heavy addictions, such as dependence on religion or spirituality, and interdependence, taking care of others at the expense of self.

When this woman refused to continue to bear the anger of her husband and tied up the fry, I saw that this model ended completely with a couple. The husband of this client is always very angry. He often loses his temper without thinking of the consequences. She would acquiesce to his angry demands. If he yells that the barbecue is not cooked enough, she will fix him a steak. If he yelled that she did not give him enough sex, she would put on a small pajamas and show sex. However, internally, she was both injured and boiling. Whenever she succumbed to his request, she would isolate herself in the utility room and eat a lot of chocolate chip cookies or Twinkies.

This habit leads to weight problems, which in turn leads to self-shame, pain and suffering, and is constantly criticized by her husband. When she asked me if I could mend her emotional vitality boundary, she was about to leave him. We did it.

The immediate results were not satisfactory. Her husband

dashed and snarled violently until he found out that he had no results. Then, one night, he cried and asked if she would help him get help. Apparently, he was sexually abused as a child and never told anyone.

Although I often see men pushing the energy of uncomfortable emotions toward the vitality boundary of women's over-acceptance, the reverse is also true. People can also take this approach with same-sex partners, friends or children. Anyone has the ability to eliminate negative emotional energy, and anyone with a permeable or huge energy boundary can easily absorb them.

Many of us grew up in dysfunctional families, such as families characterized by alcohol or other forms of drug abuse or various forms of neglect, sexual problems, emotional or verbal abuse. These dysfunctional behaviors usually lay the foundation for unhealthy emotional vitality boundaries.

For example, although my father is led by me, my own parents are alcoholics. Night after night, he sat down to drink a martini to avoid dealing with his feelings. Because I love him, I will absorb his rejection, such as his sadness, fear and anger. I will also be grateful for the emotions of everyone else in the family. I know who is sad, who is happy, who hates his or her job (just like my father) and who doesn't like it. Afterwards, I was always full of tangled emotions and feelings that I couldn't figure out. I cannot sort out my feelings from the perspective of everyone else. Not only do I lack the necessary emotional energy to hide the feelings of others, but other irregularities at home also make me take on everything for everyone, including their thoughts, needs, dreams and responsibilities.

Lack of emotional energy can make it difficult for us to stand. Emotion is power. They are the energy in motion, or the energy that makes us move forward in life. If we absorb the emotions of others, we will become exhausted and unmotivated because we lack the motivation for our own emotions.

I once worked with a young woman who was so emotionally hurt that she couldn't even make a decision on her own. Her mother was a very wealthy woman, but she was also a helicopter mother, hovering on her daughter, so much so that she dropped her out of 13 schools in ten years because she didn't like how to treat her daughter. The fact is that whenever her daughter is a little bit grumpy, her mother will lash out at her, get angry in the house, pull her out of the school, and teach her how to be arrogant in the process. The daughter has almost no personality and has become very lazy. Why does it hurt my mother's feelings, why should I try to do anything? Any friend she made treats her like a mother, pulling the stuffing out of her. She began to react to any changes in the environment, from sunspots to slightly blooming flowers, to the emotional changes of a close friend of hers, the dog. Emotional abuse is so critical that the girl's border is a complete, confusing chaos. Fortunately, she responded to some of the skills I taught her, and she became bold enough to start treatment when she was in college.

Emotional injuries can occur in almost any situation, but these injuries are always accompanied by physical violations. For example, adults who are sexually abused as adults will not only degrade physical energetic boundaries, but also destroy emotional energetic boundaries. Adults can also be ignored for long periods of time during recovery, or have never been to the hospital after surgery.

For example, I once worked with a woman who had stage 2 bowel cancer. The swelling on her abdomen is as big as a basketball. She has been treated for many years, but the lump continues to grow. Then she remembered that when she was a child, her father would beat her in the stomach every time he was drunk. Hurting her makes him feel better. Her father literally beat his malignant tumor into her stomach, causing a malignant tumor in her body. He violated her physical limits, but the fact that no one cares-their mother and uncle who lived with them never stopped him-also hurt her emotional and emotional limits of vitality. Remember that after the abuse, she began to cry and continued to cry for a whole week.

I taught her some techniques that will be introduced in Chapter 4, and her emotional energy limit began to heal. Her body is the same. Remember to abuse and cure its powerful effect, turning a malignant mass into a benign tumor that is sufficient for removal. Abuse is an attempt to get rid of one's own negative or harmful energy and steal the positive energy of others. The inner self-thinking of the abuser: "Why should I insist on this bad feeling when others can carry this energy for me?" Rape, humiliating statements, negative aggressive behavior, and other types of dysfunction will Make holes on the energetic level of another person so that bad feelings can be deposited into the energetic system of the other person. At the same time, the abuser can also draw energy from the victim through these loopholes. "Why not help yourself achieve what I want? Look at all these beautiful energies!" Think of the inner self of the abuser. The shocked victim's resources will also be lost, which is what he or she needs to deal with the abuse. The emotional impact of abuse is usually a factor of illness, mood disorders, or any extreme situation.

Another component of the emotionally vibrant challenge is the beliefs involved. Beliefs are ideas that help us make decisions. They are basically thoughts. Emotional abuse and the resulting border failure lock in thoughts that make us believe that we are not worth, worthy or worthless. Because thoughts are full of vitality, just like feelings, our thoughts can pierce boundaries, eliminate beautiful emotions, build rigid walls in our hearts, and turn our lives into a nightmare.

We have 50,000 to 70,000 ideas every day. Of these, 40,000 to 56,000 are negative, and we know that only 100 to 300 of them are debilitating beliefs. According to Dr. Deepak Chopra, 95% of these ideas are the same every day. The HeartMath Institute, a California research organization, has studied the power of negative emotions and concluded that negative thoughts affect our hearts, leading to mild and severe dysfunction and diseases, including high blood pressure, heart attacks, digestive diseases, fatigue and Sleep disorders. On the contrary, positive emotions can create better health, social communities and prosperity. The underlined phrase is "the magnetic field of the heart", that is, electromagnetic (EMF) energy from our heart beating around our body, creating opportunities for us to share all the good things with those around us.

Essentially, emotional boundaries are tied to the boundaries of our relationships. This is our next step to heaven.

Your Relational Boundaries: Greening the World

Green is the shadow of new life, mowing, young leaves, freshness and life dreams. Green is the combination of the yellow of the sun and the blue of the heavens. It also represents the boundaries of your relationship, linking your parts to yourself, the energy fields of China and the rest of the world.

A good relationship can promote justice, fairness, honor, courage and other noble virtues. They thrive through accurate and caring communication, care and compassion. Relationships also require proper relationship boundaries, that is, the boundaries that distinguish us from others, but we also need to establish connections with others. Ideally, these energy boundaries can avoid the husband, of course, can also avoid any danger, but can provide a welcome mat for happy friends, partners and all other types of companions, and even companion animals.

We have all experienced imperfect relationships. Sometimes, we may feel as if we did not choose to join those romantic relationships. Maybe we don't. We are not responsible for who the company assigns to be our boss. We did not choose relatives or even children, at least in the sense of ordering what we wanted from the catalog. However, unless there are some distortions or distortions in our relationship boundaries, we have indeed chosen how to respond to people.

Having a strong and fluid relationship boundary is like putting our inner zipper on our inside rather than outside. Our true selves can decide when to open our hearts and let someone in, or when we open up for integration. If we are tired or need a little time, we can close ourselves a little or completely open to get the rest of what we need. Healthy relationship boundaries attract people who support our spiritual mission and core personality. Such boundaries will prevent, or even completely exclude, those who might hurt, hurt, laugh at or belittle us. When unattractive or harmful people enter our energy realm, we will remain highly vigilant. Our intuition will open. If this person is a bit negative, we will feel a tangled, a feeling, a bad feeling, and may even skip our inner heart or have a mild headache. If he or she is totally horrified, our internal signals will pull all the pauses.
Our hearts will be hammered; our bodies will vibrate. Objects

may even knock down in front of us without touching them, because our borders are emitting such strong energy signals. We may receive prophetic dreams to show us what might go wrong if we let this person into our lives, otherwise God will talk to us directly or through friends. The boundary of our relationship can protect and remind us through a specific body organ and its area: the heart. This is the most electromagnetic organ in the human body and is the key to establishing the required energy boundary to ensure that you have a supportive relationship and avoid disaster.

The strength of the heart is well documented. The magnetic field generated by its magnetic field is 5,000 times the magnetic field generated by the brain, and the electric field is 60 times the magnetic field generated by the brain. The magnetic field of the heart can be measured from a few feet away from the body. This small, fist-sized organ will be greatly affected by different emotions and relationships, and the most positive relationships will produce measurable health results in every area of your body and mind. In addition, the heart's electromagnetic field (we call it your relationship field) interacts with other people's heart fields to transmit feelings and even synchronize the heartbeat, even if these people are not present.

The HeartMath Institute has proven that the electromagnetic field generated by the heart penetrates every cell of the human body and actually synchronizes each cell with each other. In fact, your heart rhythm produces "fields", which are so strong that they can change the cells and DNA of the baby in the mother's womb.

Positive relationship boundaries ensure that we have a happy social life, a caring community and good friends. It is a well-known fact that people with affectionate communities live longer, happier, and prosperous lives than those who are alienated. They also have fewer heart diseases and are healthier overall.

When love is the center, the heart produces hormones and other chemicals that support our optimal health on all levels. All of this is possible because the heart is a field, not just an organ. When people touch, approach each other or even think about each other, one person's heart signal affects another person's brain rhythm and emotions. This means that our heart field or relational energy field carries vital relational information. In fact, the message from the heart will tell people how to treat you.

If, as the ancient philosopher Sophocles once said, the word "love" "frees us from all the burdens of the world and the pain of life", then if there is no warmth, including the boundary of relationship, we are destined to move towards in contrast.

WHAT COMPROMISES OUR RELATIONAL BOUNDARIES?

I used to date a guy who seemed very friendly, but in my mind, certain things about him were wrong. He knows many of my other friends, and I don't see any logical reason to perceive the problem. One day, one of his best friends came to me.

"Hurricane Katrina, I want to warn you," he said. "He is not a good person."

My friend has no evidence, but for a long time he suspected that the person I dated might be despicable or cruel. This suggestion is correct, so I broke up with my new boyfriend that night.

My heart knew something was wrong from the beginning, but when I didn't listen immediately, my heart jumped into a messenger, forcing me to listen. Appropriate relationship boundaries will show us the true nature of another person or a group, and they will help us if we are not obedient. The problem is that our relationship boundaries are not always fail-safe. In the case of inflexible borders, we may be too isolated. It's too messy, like when our borders are spotless; or simply broken, for example when we have holes or diagonal lines in the fields.

Any or all of these situations caused us to encounter problems. Maybe we meet and get married again and again, or we always have a nasty boss. Perhaps we will continue to attract people in need, who love to let us repair our lives, but to no avail. Maybe everyone in our lives drinks Coke on vacation, and activity and productivity overwhelm us. If we are psychologically sensitive, we will understand every emotion, activity or need for the living and dead, but no one will take care of us. Healers are usually the worst, because there are people everywhere in the world, and they are willing to put their problems into other people's energy fields and steal love in return. Those of us who are sensitive to the environment will feel that we have our own lives everywhere, but we lack the power to help people large and small.

Without healthy relationship boundaries, we will fall into at least one energetic speed trap, and then every detail in life will become a questionable issue. At the most common level, we cannot even accurately assess the authenticity of the words, gestures, or thoughts of another person or a group. We don't know who to trust, what to trust, and when to trust.

We all sit next to a person, listening to his or her wax figure of us in a poetic way, perhaps complimenting how good we look, or how good we do on a project. What if you don't know if the person is telling the truth or stretching his legs? What if the wrong evaluation is made due to the distortion of the relationship field? You can make a friend who made you lose your job, marry someone who stole all your money, or hand your child to an abusive nanny.

What can break the boundaries of our relationships so that we will attract or suffer difficult, hurtful relationships instead of pleasant, supportive relationships? The heartbreaking list of complaints is too long to even start, which is a tragedy in itself. We just need to watch the evening news to see children with flying limbs and swollen abdomens, women who are raped or rejected because they want to express their opinions on foot when walking to a store, and men or walkers who are used as money-making machines. In our own homes, exposure to addiction, humiliation, emotional or physical abuse, greed, manipulation, racism, and even constant indifference make our interpersonal boundaries not expect love. We are born with intact hearts, but few people can spend their childhood wholeheartedly, much less.

If you reduce the causes of heart disease and relationship boundary damage to one word, it will be negative.

As already discussed, the Heart Mathematics Institute shows that negative emotions are the basis for most of our stress, and stress itself is the cause of most diseases (from heart disease to anxiety). Even at work, negative emotions are one of the main reasons for dissatisfaction and stress for everything from serious illness to relationship breakdown, as Steven Brown and Thomas Leigh recently published in the Journal of Applied Psychology in 1996 learn". When people are treated badly, for example, when they are subjected to harsh humor and suspicion, they become anxious, fearful, intolerant and desperate.

If we were abused as a child, grew up or went to school in an unfavorable environment, or were forced to work in the same environment, then our relationship energy boundaries were violated. I believe that all of us have wounds on the boundaries of relationships, because we naturally need relationships to survive and develop, but negative relationships are inevitable. The good news is that we aim to respond to love, which means that we can repair and recover wounds in love. But always, we must be willing to return to love, and doing so is the focus of our relationship work in this chapter.

Your Spiritual Boundaries: Peace on Earth

We are here to experience the spiritual existence of physical reality. Isn't this a grand event worth celebrating? Unfortunately, most of us are taught that the everyday world is less holy than the heavenly world. The fact is that the whole earth is a beautiful altar, but one must choose wisely the path of living in a divine and happy way. And wisdom is often hard-won.

Our spiritually vibrant boundaries are also a kind of protection and goal, which is the key to awakening our ability to treat all things (not just certain things) as spiritual things, regardless of their appearance. Colored in transparent white, this group of energy fields surrounds all other high-energy boundaries. You can think of it as your first line of defense. This is a layer of defense that asks you: "Does this incoming energy match my spiritual self?" This query is accompanied by another question: "My internal Is the energetic message that is generated to convey my truth to the world? "If healthy, our spiritual boundaries will reflect the spiritual essence of our constant inspiration, let it show our spiritual strength and talents, and spread love to the world. In many ways, these are the most important of all fields because they clarify our true identity and help us become who we should be.

Many religions believe that we are the closest to God in designated places of worship, but we should not be filled with ourselves or the greater spirit only in church or when people are watching. We are here as beings in the sky, transforming this world into a part of the paradise it was created into. There is no right or wrong way to do this, there is only the way of love or not. Not only are the number of doors leading to Absolute limited, but many of us believe there are. Therefore, our spiritual boundary is both a ladder to the heaven we are creating, and a barrier to keep us safe while we understand ourselves.

If our spiritual boundaries are intact, then no matter what our living conditions are, we will understand ourselves as spiritual people. Whether we are sick or healthy, depressed or happy, whether in close relationships or living alone, we recognize ourselves as part of the spiritual family of life and the dead, tangible and intangible, natural and supernatural. We will be assured of grace, the best goal of life, or peace in anything.

In practice, we will also accept the fact that we are on this planet for a specific purpose this time. This is a spiritual mission to be accomplished by ourselves. Our purpose does not have to be majestic before the eyes of the world. Nor should we show vigor or religiousness. Our spiritual tasks may include mothers or fathers for our clients or inner children within the clients. We may live by figures or carved tombstones. Purposeful expression has nothing to do with our means of livelihood. About how we can be what we can be.

As we strive to achieve our goals every day, we will understand God more personally. We awakened our intuitive talents and learned to master everything humane, from losing our temper to paying bills on time.

What Compromises Our Spiritual Boundaries?

Broken or injured mental energy boundaries can have almost any type of negative impact on life, including illness (physical and mental), poverty, debt, depression, anxiety and phobias. The most common mental border violations include:

- Religious sin and humiliation; for example, a woman who grew up in a church does not allow women to speak

- Spiritual intolerance; for example, being told that your views are ungodly, or that views that differ from those held in your place of worship are criminal

- Inhumane spiritual standards; for example, if you engage in natural and/or humane human behavior (such as talking with someone outside a religious group or having sex in a marriage) and you are told that you are a sinner

- Cult organizations and brainwashing, for example when religious leaders have the right to make decisions for the well-being of others

- Etiquette abuse, such as abuse in Satan (actually many fundamentalist) organizations

- The doctrines of terrorism, killing, exclusion or coercion, especially when these things are said to be done in the name of God or virtue

- Discrimination, such as hearing that God only loves men, not women, or whites, not blacks

- Political pressure, such as being told that you must be a Christian to join a particular political party, or if you belong to a political party you are not a Christian

- Any information or manipulation that for some reason insists that you are and should be separated from God

- Causes a deep sense of shame, worthlessness, lack of value, powerlessness, or bad news.

Once I taught her how to establish spiritual boundaries, the voice stopped. She has no schizophrenia at all, and no prescription drugs, except for sleeping pills at night. She used her intuitive talent as an energy healer and achieved a very successful practice.

Another client suffers from severe osteoporosis, and her prescription drugs are ineffective. She is losing weight and her overall health is declining. After talking with her, I learned that she grew up in Ukraine and in a church that promoted dedication. Her explanation of this message is that to be a good person and loved one, she needs work, work, and work, often without any financial return, and without the help of people around her. She not only dedicated her energy to every living person she met, but also dedicated her energy to the dead. Every night, she is troubled by the vivid image called "saint". They marched before her, reaching out their hands for prayers and blessings. Guess what she gave them? Her bones are very marrow.

Because she is energetic in many areas of life, her body is also exhausted. Her despicable sense of shame has established a harmful energetic pattern. Once we changed her mental boundaries and used the techniques introduced in Chapter 4, she began to recover from osteoporosis and the feeling that she shouldn't be loved unless she gave up first.

Most of the cure is to get rid of the overwhelming burden so that we can have our true place in this world. From depression to courtesy sexual abuse, we can all be victims of any repetitive illness. We may be troubled by people who rely on our spiritual gifts and abilities but get nothing. We can be sure that, no matter what, we must serve something other than ourselves or others. Our job is sacrifice and execution; that is the way to heaven.

The mentally sensitive, those who are too exposed to invisible dimensions and the subtle energies of others, usually suffer the most when it comes to spiritual boundaries. Due to the lack of spiritual boundaries, the mentally sensitive will become the prey of any or all dark forces that try to infiltrate their world. Similar conditions exist for people who have no boundaries at all. They lost their energy while bearing the spiritual floats and jet power of this world and the supernatural world. The results I see most often include conditions that others might call mood disorders, attention deficit disorder (ADD), autism, schizophrenia, and bipolar disorder. Therapists with impaired or permeable mental boundaries are often forced to continue to perform their duties due to mental misunderstandings such as "helping others is good" or "helping others is a noble job, and I am also noble". However, helping others to the point where they don't have their own life or energy is not a good or noble thing. Environmentally sensitive people associated with nature and natural forces often find that all their energy is consumed to support the needs of the natural world.

All in all, our spiritual boundaries are the key to becoming our true self and the key to maintaining a world in which we know little about spiritual things. People who are sensitive to the environment and connected with the existence and power of nature will often find that all their energies are doing their best to support the needs of the natural world.

The Four Boundaries Pulled Together

Many (if not most) living conditions involve two or more vibrant boundaries. For example, weight issues usually require research in all four areas. Most people with serious weight problems have extremely loose or permeable physical boundaries, which is why their bodies exhibit their own problems, and many times they also exhibit other people's problems. These people's own emotions are often subverted by the emotions of others, and this is an emotional energy problem, and they often find that expressing their true self is a challenge, which is a relationship problem. In addition, they usually do not believe that they are really important. This is a spiritual boundary issue. As a result, they insist on too much physical matter. The diagnosis and active treatment of weight problems complicate the fact that they may stem from any or all of the syndromes described in the next chapter.

Logically, we must doubt how we should consciously regulate all four types of energy fields to create safety and happiness. Well, we don't have to. We just need to produce unity, which exists when everything that unites us unites and works harmoniously on our behalf. If we truly maintain continuity or consistency, then we can invite all people who are not ours to join the same game, so no matter what, we can express more and more kindness and love.

HEALING OUR BODIES BY HEALING OUR BOUNDARIES

Eventually you will come to understand that love heals

everything, and love

is all there is.

GARY ZUKAV

This kind of walking called life not only teaches us how to endure pain, pain, injury and trauma, but also how to create a whole in a state of collapse. This is the meaning of healing: no matter what happens in our body, we have a sense of wholeness.

The job of our vibrant boundaries is to support our body, mind and soul in the material world as complete as spiritually. Unfortunately, many of the energies that cause illness, stress, trauma, mental imbalance, and other troubles enter through our vibrant borders.

How do we do on the physical, emotional, relationship, and spiritual boundaries to ensure that we have the best health and well-being? In this chapter, I share some scientific studies that show how strengthening our vibrant boundaries can create health. I also shared various ways to relieve our seven syndromes, which will deplete our health.

The Science of Our Energetic Boundaries and Health

Our vibrant boundaries are the first line of defense for our health. If they work properly, they will deflect or transform energy that makes us feel uncomfortable. They will also release and purify our physical and mental toxins, thereby ensuring a healthier immune system and better overall health. But, as the respected researcher Dr. James Oschman explained, once our energetic fields start to sputter and work at suboptimal levels, our body systems become overburdened and must Undertake work in this field. This depletes our body and leads to mental, behavioral and emotional challenges, which can lead to cancer, diabetes, allergies, chronic fatigue syndrome, sleep problems, migraines, cardiovascular problems, infections, adrenal pressure, epilepsy, and weight problems. And asthma. Including aggressiveness, anxiety, criminal activity, depression, memory and accidents.

Oschman explained that these pulses, oscillating

electromagnetic fields and etheric fields operate like skin, protecting us from high-energy phenomena, including external EMF fields such as fluorescent lights, radiation, sunspots and other dangerous rays. They can help us convey our intentions to the world and absorb the information we receive. In our various fields, we connect with the people around us, and our relationship with people is a key indicator of health. Our personal realm is also connected to the earth's magnetic field, thus balancing and smoothing our internal systems. When our electric field is damaged, we cannot absorb or transform negative energy at all.

As you might imagine, cooperating with these areas can greatly improve our ability to cure diseases. We can even diagnose diseases by examining the energy field. Leonard Konikiewics, a special researcher at the Pennsylvania Polyclinic Medical Center, used Kirlian photography to identify 16 of 18 cystic fibrosis patients from 140 samples. He was also able to select 37 of the 48 gene carriers. Another well-known researcher, Dr. Thelma Moss, used Kirlian photography technology to accurately determine which of the 200 mice were cancerous based on the energy emitted by the tail. Stomach cells show signs of malignancy, such as fine white or gray granular shadows, while healthy tissue is clearer. Moss was able to discern the disease from mice that had never been sick, and he performed a task that posed a challenge to today's medical diagnosticians. When using the same Kirlian procedure on 6,000 Romanian soldiers, the researchers found 47 types of tumors, while the normal method found 41 types of tumors. Electrophotography is another process more complicated than Kirlian photography. In a study conducted by scientists at the Labor Protection and Health Center in Bucharest, Romania, more than 6000 people have used electrophotography to distinguish healthy tissues from unhealthy tissues.

Dr. David Sheinkin of Rockland State Hospital in New York and his colleagues showed that the exciting ability to diagnose diseases through our energy field is not limited to certain diseases. Sheinkin conducted research on patients with respiratory, gastrointestinal, and mental illnesses and determined that the field differs from disease to disease. We can not only diagnose diseases, but also predict and prevent diseases by figuring out which energy patterns describe which diseases.

Even relationships can be analyzed in an energetic way. Investigators use Kirlian photography to show that the realm of close friends is brighter and closer than that of strangers. People think that the areas of thoughts of love or kissing are also bright and connected, while the areas of thoughts that are considered unpleasant are separate. When we are friendly, people will notice because our corona is bigger than the corona of the strict people in the narrow field.

Our field is indeed our connection to the world, but as Oschman said, the things that keep us in good shape can also make us uncomfortable. Just as we can catch the flu from another person, we can also solve health problems through our energy field, because our energy boundary is part of a huge crystalline network that contains our connective tissue and our The nervous and cardiovascular system-the fiber network throughout our body.

Doctor Robin Kelly pointed out that our energy channels or meridians are located in our connective tissues. (Many researchers have proved this fact.) This tissue conducts electricity through collagen molecules arranged in a triple helix. These collagen molecules conduct electricity through the water molecules on the cell surface. Water allows them to conduct electricity like crystals, and collagen molecules produce a certain cytoskeleton in our muscles, bones and organs. This connective tissue acts like a receiver and sender of subtle energy, it enters through our energy boundary and radiates from our energy boundary.

Our heart is the largest producer and recipient of this subtle energy. It transmits energy through the cardiovascular system to two different nervous systems: (1) Our main nervous system, which includes the spine and brain, (2)) The secondary nervous system, named by researcher Dr. Björn Nordenström, is composed of our connective tissues and meridians. Each heart pulse sends two watts of electrical energy through the blood through the connective tissue. The cells of these cells vortex like a ring-shaped vortex, a bit like a spherical doughnut. Even throwing an ion or charged particle into this mixture can generate a powerful magnetic field.

Technically speaking, the shapes of our electric and magnetic fields are different. Our magnetic field looks more like a ring, reflecting our rotating blood cells. The ring is a magical character. It looks like a doughnut, but the only part it exists is the outer surface. The vacuum does not replace the hole in the middle. This gap raises a question for quantum physicists: Are we dealing with a shape that attracts subatomic particles or waves of other sizes? The circular magnetic field from the heart is so strong that it extends to the edge of the universe.

If you cut into a donut, you will end up with two or more pieces. If you cut off a ring, you still only have one piece. This fluidity establishes a uniform magnetic field generated by a single pulse of the heart, even if the smallest displacement internally changes the rotation of our blood vessels and therefore changes our heart field.

The magnetic field of our heart is stronger than that of any other part of us. It not only extends continuously in space, but also forms a ring shape around us. After the magnetic field merges with our electric field, the electric field generates pulses from our cells in a wave-like manner. The resulting electric field is called an electromagnetic field. The combined electric field will extend outside of us (just like a separate magnetic field). The electromagnetic field also forms the uterus, constantly bathing us with our own heart energy.

The first and most important heart energy we have ever encountered is the mother's heart energy. When we are pregnant, the electromagnetic field she produces is ten to one hundred times stronger than the electromagnetic field emitted by the outside world. This sanctuary can be considered our first vibrant frontier. If supported by love, its power and strength will increase, but without that love, it will decrease. After zooming in, the field can protect us from external EMF fields, such as power lines or radiation, negative influences from others, and other dark influences. I suggest that some of our health problems and problems in other areas of life are due to insufficient protection in the womb. For example, if our mother does not want us, is not loved by others, or does not love us, it may happen to love yourself .

As discussed, our magnetic field is circular, and our electric field can be measured as pulses of varying length, width, and intensity. However, at some point, we must stop distinguishing between the magnetic and electric fields of the heart because they combine and change with each heartbeat. The EMF field goes far beyond our body, conveying our own energy information to the world, and receiving energy information from people, places, objects (all things), and sucking it back into our body.

The information collected in our fields can guide our genes, determine cell differentiation and change our health, because this information is sensitive to our DNA. At every level, our high-energy fields work like radio waves, allowing us to touch the EMF fields of others and exchange energy. This means that our energy boundary is a model of perception and communication, as well as a medium for determining and creating health. In fact,

the healthier our heart rhythm is, the healthier our body will be.
Studies have shown that a coherent or harmonious heart
produced when we are centered on positive emotions and
spiritual truth can prevent infection, improve arrhythmia and
help cure mitral valve prolapse, congestive heart failure, asthma,
and diabetes , Fatigue, autoimmune diseases, anxiety,
depression, AIDS and post-traumatic stress disorder (PTSD).

The most powerful EMF producer, a caring heart, can drive or
coordinate all body functions and organs, as well as our
emotional, mental and spiritual health, thereby creating the best
physical health. It ensures the sharing of healing energy within us
and between our heartbeats and others. It also establishes an
agreement for all our energetic borders, instructing them to allow
only those that support our overall well-being and exclude
everything that might harm us.

Healing Through Your Physical Boundaries: Your RedField

Problems in the energetic field are usually caused by touching violations (whether sexual, physical, or suggestive) or witnessing such violations. Any major trauma to the body or neglect of our basic needs can also rigidify, tear or weaken our physical boundaries, resulting in any one of the seven syndromes and any number of health conditions. Touch is not always physical. Harsh, mean words or insulting insults are considered physical aggressions because their high-energy vibrations can penetrate our body boundaries and harm our tissues.

For example, I was aware of my mother's womb before I was born, and I still remember the angry words exchanged between mother and father. The sound waves from their "discussion" will spin into my body, scorching my ego. I can feel these sounds both psychologically and physically. Since then, those angry words hit all of my places in the womb. Since then, I have had physical problems, including infections, allergies and irregular heartbeats. Arrhythmia is related to alcohol. Until I was in my forties, every night around 10 o'clock, I was troubled by arrhythmia. And midnight. Before I called my mother and a sibling and found out that I was born, my parents were drunk every night between these two hours (my relatives, including my mother, continued to drink during these hours), I have been unable to figure out the reason. Once I discover the storyline, I can release the bond between my loved ones and myself and repair my physical (and emotional and relationship) realm. The arrhythmia disappeared. In the end, I found myself suffering from Healer's Syndrome. I am absorbing the toxic energy of my parents and responding with love, losing my body in the process.

If we are really struggling with physical illness, it is important to find the root cause. Using the "Discover Storyline" exercise in Chapter 4, you can search for original violations, people, words, phrases, or trauma, and find the syndromes that affect you. You may also want to explore situations where you should be touched, clasped or raised but not touched. Neglect also constitutes a violation. Once you discover the source conflict, it is important to forgive yourself for "allowing" energetic injuries to happen and happen again. Under pressure, we unknowingly do anything necessary for survival. The initial strategy is rarely effective in the long term, but we stick to this model because it seems to be at least helpful. Forgiving yourself for reacting in a way that hurts us or others is not about accepting blame. It's about understanding our motivation for establishing a vitality model. Once we forgive ourselves, this pattern will disappear. Then, when we are ready to forgive other people involved, our job is complete. The pattern usually disappears or can be treated.

Forgiving others does not mean approving abuse. Rather, it means returning their energy to them so they can deal with it, and we no longer need to do that. In every situation, every energy, good or bad, has a gift. Even if it is dark and negative energy, for us, it is not necessary to grasp the energy of others, because that person cannot open the gift contained in it.

I always return the energy of others to their higher selves, or pass it on to the divine power, instead of passing it on to other people directly. It is difficult for me to learn. I once had a client who committed suicide for decades. We are sure that her father's wish to die has entered her own system through her physical field. We vigorously returned this wish to her father, and he committed suicide the next day.

As a healer, I now only send energy through higher channels, so it will have a love effect instead of an acute effect. I asked God to connect everyone involved with his or her own healing grace. The stream of healing grace surrounds and radiates. Essentially, they are energetic hearts. The existence of these facts means that we don't have to win this grace/love, but just allow it. To heal your energy boundaries, you only need to connect yourself to a healing stream prepared for you; to heal others or prevent them from penetrating your boundaries will invite them to use your own healing stream.

Then, I asked God to release negative or intrusive energy from my client and return it to another higher self. This process applies to illness, death wish, curse, rope, physical release, and all other issues. Finally, I ask my client to accept the recovery of physical or physical boundaries.

Below are other tools to support health and recovery through the energetic boundaries of the body.

Because our body responds to substances, I suggest that you program food and beverages deliberately. You can use exercises to set intent (in Chapter 4) to perform this process. To rebuild the boundaries of the body, please bless your protein and minerals. The chakras associated with physical energy boundaries are highly physical and are strengthened in nature. As far as the glands are concerned, you are dealing with the adrenal glands and bones. These systems require large amounts of healthy protein and minerals. If possible, only eat grass-fed, free-range animal meat, because these animals are more willing if they are unknowingly willing to serve. If you eat meat that has been slaughtered and processed in commercial slaughterhouses and meat packaging plants, then you will feel fear and further hurt your borders. Liquid minerals and vitamins are easier to program as you wish than powders or solids. As mentioned in the science class at the beginning of this chapter, water can conduct electricity. Minerals are ions, so they can enhance your EMF field. Intentionally programming minerals can further enhance your physical boundaries.

When assessing your physical field visually, check its brown and red hues, as these are the colors associated with the corresponding chakras. Check for spots or invasive colors, spots, holes, gaps or areas that are too thick or too large. Also look for ropes and other dynamic accessories. Then start to fix the fields on the screen in your mind, add colors or delete colors as needed.

Countless kinds of gems and metals can be programmed to improve your physical health and well-being. My favorite is ruby, which is considered a sacred gem for curing diseases. Red provides support for your first chakra, which creates an auroral field around and around your body. The first auroral layer is one of the two layers that constitute what I call the physical energy boundary. The other tenth lug layer related to the tenth chakra. Please refer to the chart provided in "Central Area: Chakras and Your Energy Boundaries" on page 104 to understand the chakra you are dealing with and its associated auroral field. Then you can choose metals and gems accordingly.
Using shapes, sounds, and numbers can significantly change the

vibration of your blood cells, as you recall, they rotate in a circle, which creates our electromagnetic field. Changing the strength, direction and momentum of blood cell rotation can change the function of the physical force field. The most basic tones used are Hindu Lam and C octave. The main number is 1, although if you want to change it, try using 10. For the shape, I found it very helpful to use spirals, which mimic the circular motion of blood cells and magnetic fields.

Think about the specific disease or condition you encountered, recall the storyline, and ask Shenzhou to help you perceive the energy (or syndrome) that caused this problem. Now, imagine that negative or intrusive energy is spinning in red, counterclockwise, and asking God to release it out of your body and energetic realm. Next, ask God to bring beneficial energy into your vision and body through a clockwise golden spiral. In the process, you will release physical toxins and energy that do not exist in your body, and attract higher harmonic gold.

Miasms and Vivaxis ropes are energy issues related to physical energy fields, but have nothing to do with other boundaries.

Dispersion is a high-energy mode intertwined in our physical energy field. They are related to the tenth chakra, but are actually programmed into epigenetic chemicals that surround our genes and preserve the memories, emotions and experiences of our ancestors. Migraine is a disease pattern. We are born with a specific pattern woven in the epigenetic soup and physical energy field (especially a part of it called the morphogenetic field, which is a certain type of energy field that connects us to other people). This means that the energetic boundaries of our cells and bodies have incentives for certain diseases (whether physical or mental illness) or certain traumatic events (such as accidents or abuse).

Vivaxis is a cord similar to an umbilical cord, which enters near our belly button and attaches to the ground where we were born or nearby. With Vivaxis, we send energy to and receive energy from that geographic location. Unless the actual land is poisoned, this exchange can sustain life. My Dutch-Canadian client (the case I described in the "Environmental Syndrome" section of Chapter 3) is an example of a person who suffered from Vivaxis disease between the borderline of her vigorous body and the toxic farm where she was born. inverted.

By visually reading our physical boundaries, we can discover diffuse disease or inappropriate Vivaxis connections. The deadlock looks like a web of interlocking and pulsating. If we also examine these spots, we will see the same grid around the genes in the epigenetic fluid. Another way to find out if you have depression is to explore your family tree. What disease patterns are present? If there are recurring themes (or worse, if you are affected by family patterns), you are likely to experience depression. Low mood can make you adapt to any of the seven syndromes, and it is itself a vampire energy that can feed the ancestor (or the spirit of the ancestor) who initially established the model.

Vivaxis looks like a rope, in my opinion, it is like a garden hose, but bigger. It will be inserted into the abdomen, like a tree trunk, extending the roots into your body. You can judge whether it is poisoned or not based on the color of the energy entering the body through these roots. If the energy is black, moldy brown or dirty red, you need to remove Vivaxis because this land sends you negative energy. If your own energy is also absorbed, then you will fall into a strange "healer syndrome", instead of serving humans or others, but serving the environment.

Using a variation of the exercise "Discover Storyline", you can heal two energetic anomalies. In this case, you are discovering someone else's storyline, not your own storyline. If you experience pain, let God show you what happened to the ancestor who initiated the pain. Tragic events usually occur, such as death, famine, relentless marriage, disease or disaster, which causes disease. In the case of Vivaxis, please ask the land to tell you what happened and why it asked for your help.

In both cases, Shenzhou was asked to heal the initial problem. Even if your ancestor has been dead for centuries, ask his ancestors for help. If this pattern continues, then the souls of your ancestors will not calm down. Heal your ancestors and then receive the same treatment for everyone in your bloodline (including yourself and your children). Insert therapeutics where you need to correct your genes, epigenetic chemicals and physical energy fields. For Vivaxis, ask God to heal this land by establishing a flow of healing grace for it. Ask for another healing grace to enter your system instead of Vivaxis, invite this love to thoroughly cleanse and repair your body, chakras and physical fields. You can also port Vivaxis to new locations, such as your favorite locale, your current residence, or even heaven.

Healing Through Your Emotional Boundaries: Your Orange Field

One study after another shows that emotions make us sick.

Whenever we fall into a negative emotional state, we create conditions for physical and mental illness. The feeling of being stuck for a long time, especially the feeling that we have not processed, can damage our neuropeptides, which promote communication between various parts of the body. Then we become disconnected from ourselves, and this disconnection can cause alienation and disease. For example, if excessive anger is not expressed in a harmless manner, it can lead to heart disease, drug and alcohol addiction, headaches, domestic violence and depression. Constant fear pumps cortisol and other hormones into the body, causing cell failure and more stress. Incurable sadness and sorrow are the root causes of deep depression, and shame and guilt are often the basis of addiction. And self-deception, the other half of the emotional equation, prepares us for stress and wrong decisions.

There are four main ways to deal with stress: fight, run away, freeze or feel. Only the last one will lead to growth and transformation, but if you suffer from any of the seven syndromes, especially those that cause you to absorb the feelings of others, it will be difficult for you to get your own feelings and related beliefs. Therefore, the first step to heal the emotional realm is to distinguish one's own emotions from those of others. The second step is to use a variety of dynamic tools to restore your emotional boundaries. The third step in progress is to mature your feelings and beliefs.

How do you separate your emotions from the emotions of others and release your emotions? First read your emotional domain carefully. You want to perceive healthy, sunny orange energy light (because orange and yellow are the colors of the second and third chakras). Anything else, you are likely to lose energy, take on the energy of others, lack the necessary boundaries and/or be invaded by outside forces.

When working in the emotional realm, I usually trace damage or deformation to the chakras, especially when I feel the color is missing or missing. If there is a complete lack of orange, you may suppress your feelings. If your vision lacks orange and has too much yellow, you may be dealing with autism spectrum disorder or attachment disorder. Attention deficit/hyperactivity disorder (ADHD) usually involves the third chakra and emotional boundary of burnout, where there is too much yellow, which means you are absorbing too much information from outside yourself. If the content of oranges is too low, it means that you are thinking too much and feeling insufficient. For both cases, please refer to Chapter 2 and the discussion about crystal souls.

When checking your emotional field, you should also pay special attention to the damage that leads to the syndrome. Vulnerabilities indicate the possibility of vampire, M child or healer syndrome. Ropes and accessories can cause mental sensitivity and borderless syndrome. Too much environmental information indicates environmental syndrome. Repeated symbols, images or patterns are the psychological signs of Paper Doll Syndrome. Identifying what is happening will help you rebuild your emotional realm.

Ask God to replace all energies that are not yourself (whether these energies are only emotional, only spiritual, or a combination of the two) with a stream of healing grace. (The "spiritual to spiritual" technique provided in Chapter 4 is a good way to separate and release the emotional energy of others.) It also requires your emotions and beliefs (emotions and beliefs related to and related to your spiritual self) to become alive And easy to obtain.

You may need days, weeks, or even months to integrate changes. Sometimes, we don't want to let the feelings of others cloud our own feelings, because we don't want to feel our own pain. (Sometimes you don't have to feel and process your own feelings. This is the reward for establishing an active pattern of the syndrome.) If this process of change becomes intense, I recommend working with a therapist, especially using a vibrant one such as EMDR Tools of the therapist (desensitize and reprogram the movement of the eyes), regression, light therapy or color therapy, sound therapy or acupuncture points to achieve rehabilitation. Medical Qigong is an ingenious way to make life energy move through our body. It is also very useful, such as receiving massage and other therapeutic car bodies.

Now is the time to separate your feelings from your beliefs and mature the two. To mature our emotions and beliefs is to respect and follow the information inherent in them so that they can make us happy. (See "Information in Our Emotions and Beliefs.")

Psychologically check your emotional realm to express your feelings intuitively. Current or healthy anger is usually seen as red; sadness is blue; fear is yellow; the offensive healthy version is bright gray, which means that something or someone is not suitable for us. Delight is any version of bright orange or clear and bright primary colors.

Any discoloration indicates an emotional problem. When we judge that a feeling is bad, others do the same thing, or we hold other people's energy, color distortion occurs. The old anger or the anger of other people will become red, brown or black. Black usually indicates a form of depression. The closer we are to the ebony, the greater our anger. Anger is a deep hurt, a combination of pain and anger. The sadness of being ignored or others is dark blue and moody. If we waste our energy on other people, the leakage area may be light blue.

Long-term fear will appear in the form of unstable, crazy yellow oscillations. If it represents suppressed fear or the fear belongs to another person, the yellow will turn brown; if the fear has been externalized, the yellow will turn pale yellow. The more the yellow color changes, the more anxiety is expressed.

Unhealthy disgust, shame, blame or guilt will be offensive gray. These spots also look moldy and may be connected by wires to the person who hurt and humiliated us in the first place.

Using color repair, we can remove negative colors and fill vibrant areas (and chakras) with healthy colors. I also suggest chanting the Indian tones Vam and Ram and the octave tones D and E to enhance our emotional healing ability. These can point to the second and third chakras respectively. We can also mentally insert any version of the numbers 2 and 3 into our energy field.

In addition to evaluating the colors of our emotional boundaries, you can also use your mental vision to find shapes that are stuck in your field. Distorted or ingrained squares indicate depression or depression. The dotted circle tells you the causal relationship caused by interpersonal relationships, and the triangle deformation indicates anxiety. X represents an energy mark, or the location of a rope or curse. The spirit part of this chapter discusses how to deal with these types of interference. Usually, repairing deformed symbols can enhance your emotional realm and help you understand more clearly the true nature of your feelings and thoughts.

Good gems that can be used for emotional therapy include: marine jasper, which can release the emotions of others from your realm; and iron mica, which can promote emotional recovery.

All these strategies support the true purpose of emotions and beliefs: to lead us into joy. Once you feel a strong sensation, isolate it. Ask God to help you figure out the message behind this feeling. It also asks what you should do, thinking or believing to turn it into happiness. Do the same for your ideas. Especially when you are in trouble, ask the gods to point out beliefs that will destroy your happiness. Now, turn it into a more lasting belief, a true fact. Thoughts such as "I don't deserve to be healthy" may be open to the healing that God brings me. "

THE MESSAGES WITHIN OUR FEELINGS AND BELIEFS

There are five main sense constellations or groupings. All other feelings fall into these categories, and each of these five feelings conveys a specific message to us. If respected, it will bring joy.

- **Sadness** Tell us that we are out of touch with love. If we follow our grief, we will rediscover the happiness we once loved and be able to love again. Where there is love, joy overflows.

- **Anger** Indicates a violation of the boundary. Someone (or something) violated our boundaries, or we did it to other people. We need to set boundaries for ourselves and protect ourselves from others when necessary. Constant anger creates structure and therefore the joy of safety. Happiness only expands in terms of safety.

- **Fear** Tell us that we or someone or other things are in danger. We need to move forward, backward or to one side or the other. Fear urges us to take action and provides us with enough space to decide what brings joy.

- **Disgust** Implying that someone or a certain behavior, behavior or substance is harmful to us. Getting rid of or getting rid of toxins can purify us. It changes the shame and inner feelings, and enables us to fly forward, looking for people and environments that can bring us joy.

- **Joy** Say, "I want more of the same things." Joy brings more joy!

Faith is the basis of our decision-making. Just like feeling, any belief can lead to joy and productive emotions, but only if we are willing to restructure destructive beliefs so that they support unity and unity, rather than separation and disharmony.

There are six types of misunderstandings that can lead us astray and destroy our emotional boundaries. These problems include: (1) unworthy, (2) unlikable, (3) unworthy, (4) lack of value, (5) bad or evil, and (6) powerless problems. Energetic is that these unexplored beliefs lock in our brains and run our neurochemical reactions, causing destruction on our emotional energy boundaries. The people and situations they attract reinforce immature beliefs rather than encourage growth and change. Printing one of these beliefs on our emotional boundaries is like wearing a sign that spreads one's lie.

To change destructive beliefs, we must first isolate them. Once you understand the misunderstanding, don't humiliate yourself. We are dealing with an incomplete or immature belief, which is not a bad belief. Teenagers are not failed adults; they are just underage children. Just as it is our job to teach young people how to think more clearly, it is also our job to transform immature beliefs into a more mature version of ourselves. In this way, we no longer cultivate faith, but cultivate faith to make it useful, not harmful.

Shame is a form of control. When someone hurts us, especially when we are young, we have two choices. Either we must believe that the other person is injured and does not know how to love, or we must believe that abuse is our fault. The first option makes us feel helpless and hopeless. We would rather feel overwhelmed than overwhelmed. The second option is wrong, but it makes us feel that we can still control the situation. If we change, the situation may change. In order to avoid any kind of opinion, please tell yourself: "I can love myself, love myself, and love others because of who they are now." Healing through relationship boundaries: your green field

Healing your relationship field is the most effective way to create a healthy condition, because your heart (the control center of the field) can also manage the rest of your body. As discussed at the beginning of this chapter, it also generates the most expansive and interactive electromagnetic field.

Although interpersonal relationships are the source of most of our boundary injuries, they are also the key to recovery. I believe people are good at their core. As human beings, we emphasize "kindness" and we desire to be loved and loved. Love can heal and create health. A Yale University study conducted by cardiologist Dean Ornish showed that men and women who feel loved and supported have fewer heart arteries blocked. In fact, in a study of 10,000 people, men who felt that their wives did not love them were twice as likely to suffer from angina. As an interesting study conducted by the Soviets shows, love is also contagious. This research was relayed by the physicist William Tiller in his book "Science and Human Change", revealing that two hearts can be connected through a relationship field even when they are separated from each other. The Soviets took two animal hearts from their respective corpses, placed them in different rooms, and kept the hearts in a stable state. Then place the heart at the focal point of the elliptical mirror, so that any subtle radiation leaving one heart will be received by the other, and vice versa. Initially, the two hearts beat at different rhythms, but over time, their heartbeats synchronize.

Thiele believes that humans establish these connections through our hearts, especially our heart chakras and related energy fields. The greater the signal power of the larger frequency band (or bandwidth), the more people we are approaching and approaching. The finer the power signal and the narrower the bandwidth, the fewer people we can contact, and then it can only be a close-up shot. Guess what caused the large signal and huge bandwidth? The most loving connection? Love. Tiller pointed out that the attitude of trial and negative attitude reduces our inner signals and closes our vibrant areas. This also makes it difficult for people to feel any love being sent to us. Can you imagine what would happen if we actually intended to send or receive love through our relationship field?

If it can be cured through our relationship field, why do many of us get sick? The reason is that most of us are usually injured in childhood, and our injured inner child maintains a relationship boundary that seems to be protective but not protective. The inner child thinks that he or she can only survive by sticking to known methods, releasing energy, absorbing the energy of others, or connecting with negative spirits. She or he is convinced that security lies in removing borders, interdependence or being too unified with the environment. In order to truly heal from health challenges, including mental and emotional illnesses and addictions, we need to provide food for our inner children. Once he or she is rejuvenated, our relationship field will automatically begin to refresh and renew. At that time, we can carry out a variety of dynamic technologies to expand our relationship field. Some of these techniques can also help us find and help injured children.

You may find some of the techniques in Chapter 1 useful. They aim to help parents live with their children, but they can also help adults live with their inner children. Treatment and the twelve-step procedure are also crucial. In order to work energetically, I suggest you focus on the syndrome that is causing you the most trouble, and perform the "Reveal Storyline" exercise in Chapter 4. This exercise will help you figure out why your inner child is trapped in the deformation of the relationship field. After establishing contact with the injured child, please continue to care and care. A physical therapist can educate you on how to re-raise this little child, but for the purpose of physical rehabilitation, here are some useful tips.

First, redesign your relationship field. If you are suffering from a physical illness or injury, please add green to your mind; if your core problem is essentially relationship-related, such as social phobia or abuse, please add pink. If the most obvious symptom is chronic, repetitive, or addictive, add gold; if your problem is a mental one (associated with an entity or attachment); or if you have no boundaries at all. You can also combine these colors.

Now, let God connect your inner child with the healing grace, and then insert the same grace into your relationship realm. Ask Divine to fill this field (and surround the children) with the appropriate hue, intensity, and heart color just described. Knowing that this incoming energy will push out all the unwanted energy. Allow this healing flow and incoming energy to continue to flow when necessary.

If your problem is a physical problem, you can also visually depict the square of the entire field; this shape will keep you safe until you heal. If your challenge is relational in nature, use circles. If you encounter difficulties, try using triangles.

Any green gem can be used to repair physical problems through the boundary of the relationship. Green jade has strength and protection, and is very suitable for pairing with squares. Malachite and rose quartz help the body heal and care for others, and they work well together. You can buy jewelry with a round stone shape, or you can attach a round shape to jewelry, such as a pendant on a pendant bracelet. Emerald green tourmaline can purify the energy on each boundary and strengthen our inner spirit, releasing the energy of others, including the energy from physical and spiritual attachment.

The heart is especially useful for Hindu-sound yam and the immortal Om. The octave F provides a healing effect, and the number 4 provides safety. If your energetic problem is based on communication, such as you were initially hurt by verbal threats, criticism, or mental interference, then in addition to the number 5, you can also use the fifth chakra ham and G tone. Communication questions can also be responded to programmed chrysocola, lapis lazuli and blue opal.

The heart chakra symbol enhances our healing power and

related energy field because it contains several important symbols: the twelve-petal lotus, circle and triangle (two superimposed on each other). The innermost symbol represents the mantra or the sound "yam".

The twelve petal lotus is another powerful tool to heal the physical condition through the boundary of the relationship. In Hindu tradition, the symbol of the heart chakra is two overlapping triangles set in a circle, and both triangles are surrounded by lotus petals. A triangle is on the upper right; the other points fall. These different directions symbolize a choice: we will either arouse unconditional feelings of love and dedication, or we will fall into despair and negativity. The twelve petals of the lotus flower represent higher virtues that can cheer us up: love, understanding, peace, harmony, sympathy, blessing, clarity, unity, sympathy, kindness, purity and forgiveness. The circle reflects unity and perfection.

To meditate on this lotus flower, take a deep breath. Then, with each breath, focus on one of the twelve virtues and the uplifting spirit of love. Breathing into each of the virtues or lotus petals will fill your heart with positive emotions and healing. I suggest that you depict your inner child in this lotus every day and cover it with your relationship area. Now, imagine the twelve virtues as a flow of energy that shines into and through the relationship field around the inner child, holding and protecting him or her.

Laughter and inner smile also help to heal your heart and relationship areas. They are particularly interesting and dynamic tools. By lowering the levels of the stress hormones adrenaline, cortisol, dopamine and adrenaline, and human growth hormone, laughter can strengthen your immune system and reduce stress. It can also increase the levels of healthy hormones, such as endorphins and neurotransmitters. When you laugh, your body produces healthy antibodies and T cells.

Combine laughter with the work of the inner child by making a joke to the inner child. Let the sense of humor flow through your body and energy field and see how quickly your health changes.

If you can't laugh a lot, you can consider the inner smile, the open technique of Taoism and the noble energy of joy. The respected monk Thich Nhat Hanh taught us how to get an inner smile. First, sit up your spine, but don't get stiff. Relax your body, breathe, and focus on specific parts of your body. (You can choose a stressful area.) Now breathe and smile at that part of the body. You can simply imagine the smile in your heart, or you can make your face smile at the same time. There are about 300 muscles on your face, and when we worry, they harden. However, when we breathe while smiling, the tension disappears immediately and increases our happiness. French physiologist Israel Waynbaum (Israel Waynbaum) proved that a deep smile triggers specific brain neurotransmitters, such as endorphins and immune-boosting T cells. It also reduces stress hormones, cortisol, adrenaline and norepinephrine, and produces hormones that stabilize blood pressure, relax muscles, improve breathing, relieve pain, accelerate healing, and stabilize mood.

Healing Through Your Spiritual Field: Your White Boundaries

The client said: "I am sick because I am sick."

Over the years, Joanne has experienced a series of problems, including chronic fatigue syndrome, depression, borderline personality disorder, anxiety and general malaise. Even if she loves her husband, two children and a job, she feels lonely and lonely. She just feels bad about herself or her life. Her only excitement came from being chased by dark angels in her night dream. It wasn't until she worked hard to resolve the mental boundaries of malnutrition that Joanna's emotional and mental health barriers were eliminated.

Although our current symptoms may be related to health, we will know when we need to work in the spiritual field rather than in other fields. We will feel that our health problems stem from events, entities or energies that are more natural than nature. From the bottom of our hearts, we will understand that the root of external problems is about our purpose, value, value, relationship with God, sense of kindness, and our own soul. Our soul is the part of us that travels through time and space, accumulating gifts and injuries. Every soul is affected by the trauma of the original soul, which creates a spiritual misunderstanding. This trauma on the soul often becomes the foundation of our childhood.

If I think the client is dealing with mental problems, I usually start by looking for the original soul trauma. Then, I support this process by performing spiritual boundary work. Any mental illness can be caused by violation of mental boundaries, but the most common are mental illnesses, such as borderline personality disorder, paranoia, and bipolar disorder; learning problems; sleep problems; depression; and anxiety. Psychotherapy almost always involves dealing with ropes, entities, attachments, and other spiritual invasions. Therefore, sensitivity syndrome is almost always a part of mental discomfort.

For example, I believe that bipolar disorder usually starts with a split soul. Characterized by severe mood swings, this bipolar person usually has mental misunderstandings, such as: "If I do something wrong, God will not love me." The soul cannot do the right thing forever, and the brain is split. In two parts. One aspect of thinking is the self that can't do wrong, that is, the perfect, happy, and attractive "good self." On the other hand is the "bad self", which is the despicable, cruel and crazy self that we often become ruthless. Due to mental misunderstandings, bipolar people have to reject their bad self, so they can never be cured.

It is a group of spiritual entities that often fuels dark spiritual beliefs. They actively want to absorb our unfavorable aspects because they do not want our favorable aspects to achieve their spiritual goals. But because of the lack of the power restrained by our dark side, the bright side cannot accomplish anything.

My assessment of mentally induced borderline personality disorder is similar to that of bipolar disorder, except that the patient is hijacked by one of his own inner children rather than by an entity (although entities may also exist). Schizophrenia is usually caused by doubts about God's protection and love. The resulting fear will cause the human soul to crawl out literally; when the soul rushes over the head (seventh chakra) and hangs in the spiritual realm, true schizophrenia occurs.

To deal with any physical or mental condition of this similar group of people, medical treatment, treatment and nutritional support are required. However, if we are really dealing with spiritual issues, and therefore spiritual boundary issues, these activities alone will not solve the problem. To truly heal, we must expose our initial soul trauma; challenge and change our spiritual misunderstandings; release any negative attachments, such as those that connect us with entities or evil creatures; and repair our spiritually vibrant boundaries. The following is a meditation process that can help you achieve all these goals. I encourage you to also seek professional help for such issues.

HEALING A SOUL WOUND

To heal the wound of the soul, you must first find it. I recommend using the "discover the storyline" exercise and let yourself drift as early as possible. Although your soul may have been hurt in this life, it may be scarred for the first time in a previous life or when it was separated from your spirit. Allow yourself to re-experience the original trauma, and then ask a genius doctor to treat you from Chinese medicine and provide you with help and boundary support until you are fully recovered again.

Also know that you may find that different parts of the soul are scattered in different times, spaces and lives, or even wandering between lives. Ask God to summon all parts of your soul and stitch them together through love, cleansing, healing and fusing them together. In fact, many mental health diseases are the result of broken souls, and once we are healthy, they will begin to heal.

Releasing Cords and Other Attachments. See

Chapter 3 for information on ropes and energy accessories. Then check your mental energy field to determine which type will affect you. You may also want to trace the attachment into your body and find out in which chakra it is hooked. Finding this charka-attachment point will tell you more about why the wire exists and who is connected to you.

In addition to wires, look for any energy marks, they look like a big X. This X is usually written in your spiritual realm, facing outwards. It tells people how to treat you, which is usually not a good thing.

To release power cords, energy restraints, or markers, close your eyes and visualize your mental realm. Let Divine show you the entry point of the attachment and tell you how the attachment affects you. Check who or what the cable is connected to your outside, and where the cable is hooked in your body.

Now ask God to replace this healing stream of grace or, if necessary, to supplement several healing streams. After placing it in place, what do you need to better understand the nature of love so that attachment can be completely released. Then bless yourself and all others involved, and pray that God will continue to protect you while restoring all energetic boundaries.

You can support the restoration of the spiritual realm through prayer, meditation or meditation. Prayer conveys a message to God; meditation quiets the self so it can be answered. Contemplation is like drinking tea with God; we can sit there forever, gazing into God's eyes, basking in this eternal existence, and just enjoying our own nature.

Saying Hindu Om or octave A or B supports spiritual boundary repair. Various stones may also be useful. Diamonds are always the soul's best friend, who can clarify and clear diamonds. Moldavite (Moldavite) brings a spiritual transformation, and black opal helps to release spiritual invaders. The lapis lazuli gets a higher size to restore life, and the amber is ground after the soul is cleared. Finally, I suggest you take the time to unlock your spiritual gifts.